Today's Questions. Timeless Answers.

Looking for time-tested guidance for the dilemmas of the spiritual life? Find it in the company of the wise spiritual masters of our Catholic tradition.

Be Not Afraid

Be Not Afraid

Wisdom from John Paul II

Compiled and with a foreword by Marianne Lorraine Trouvé, FSP

BOOKS & MEDIA
Boston

Library of Congress Cataloging-in-Publication Data

John Paul II, Pope, 1920-2005.

Be not afraid : wisdom from John Paul II / compiled and with a foreword by Marianne Lorraine Trouvé , FSP.

pages cm. -- (Classic wisdom collection)

ISBN-13: 978-0-8198-1221-6

ISBN-10: 0-8198-1221-8

1. Catholic Church--Doctrines. I. Trouvé, Marianne Lorraine, editor of compilation. II. Title.

BX1378.5.J656A25 2014

242--dc23

2013045626

Scripture references and other quotations are transcribed from the original translations of John Paul II's works.

Excerpts from John Paul II's Magisterium and papal documents © Libreria Editrice Vaticana. All rights reserved. Used with permission.

Cover design by Rosana Usselmann

Cover photo: © istockphoto.com / earleliason

Published by Pauline Books & Media, 50 Saint Pauls Avenue, Boston, MA 02130-3491

Printed in the U.S.A.

www.pauline.org

Pauline Books & Media is the publishing house of the Daughters of St. Paul, an international congregation of women religious serving the Church with the communications media.

1 2 3 4 5 6 7 8 9   18 17 16 15 14

For Catherine Sparks—the best teacher I ever had,

whose example inspired me

to open the doors of my heart to Christ.

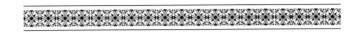

Contents

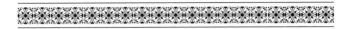

Foreword

Do you remember when Pope John Paul II was elected? I was a novice doing door-to-door evangelization in Bayonne, New Jersey, with a sister of Polish descent. When we found out that the new Pope was Polish, she just about danced for joy! The day of his death, more than twenty-six years later, is also seared in my memory. I was having lunch with some other sisters, and someone came over to tell us the Pope had just died. We stopped a moment to pray, and then spoke about how this great Pope had affected our lives.

Up to that point, I had lived my entire life as a professed sister with John Paul as Pope. During those twenty-six years, amazing things had happened, things that had previously seemed impossible. The Berlin Wall came tumbling down. The Solidarity movement in Poland started something that could not be stopped, and freedom finally came to Eastern Europe as the Iron Curtain was shattered.

In the Church, John Paul II brought a new spirit of hope. The Pope navigated a difficult course in the confusion of those post-Vatican II years. He traveled all over the world, bringing the Gospel to all peoples. I saw him twice in New York—in the Bronx at Yankee Stadium in 1979 and at Aqueduct Park, in Queens, in 1995. He radiated enthusiasm and love. He treated each person with great warmth and respect, seeing the image of God in each one.

In my work during the following years as an editor at Pauline Books & Media, I became more familiar with the Pope's writings. I am especially grateful that I was able to collaborate in the publication of several volumes of his works, in particular his masterful catechesis on the theology of the body: *Man and Woman He Created Them*. At first few people were paying attention to his general audiences on this subject. But slowly these ideas became better known and subsequently had a great impact on many people. John Paul's approach to the human person continues to resonate deeply with people today. He offers a unique view of man, woman, marriage, and the family.

That unique view was first seen when he stepped out onto the balcony to bless the crowd after his election. He stayed a long time, singing hymns in Italian, as if to assure the crowd that the first non-Italian pope in centuries would not be a stranger to them. And how many of us can still remember his final appearance at the window, just three days before he died, to bless the crowd. Frail, elderly, and showing the effects of his Parkinson's disease, he still radiated the power of his great faith. Like a father, he had spent himself to seek people out, to bring them the love of God the Father. His last words were, *"I sought you out*, and now you come to me. Thank you!"*

Born in 1920 to a devout Catholic family, Karol Wojtyla's life was marked by deep joys and intense sufferings. He lost his mother, Emilia, a month before he turned nine. His older brother, Edmund, died when Karol was twelve. As a young man he saw his world crumble when World War II broke out as the Nazis swept into Poland. Shortly after, in 1941, his beloved father died. Although Karol had felt drawn toward a career in acting, during the war he worked in a chemical plant and became a clandestine seminarian. He followed his call to the priesthood and was ordained in 1946.

As a priest he carried out an effective pastoral ministry, continued higher studies, and taught at the Catholic University of Lublin. He enjoyed working with young ople, and in dialogue with them he developed his ideas about the importance of marriage and family life. In 1958 he was ordained a bishop and fearlessly confronted the communist authorities in Poland. He took part in the Second Vatican Council and implemented the Council's reforms at home.

He was elected Pope on October 16, 1978, the first non-Italian Bishop of Rome in 455 years. From that moment he focused on leading the Church into the third Christian millennium. To that end, he traveled the world to proclaim Jesus Christ to all people, making a tremendous impact on hearts and minds and drawing large crowds everywhere he went. In his first encyclical, *Redeemer of Man,* John Paul said that the Church was in the time of a great Advent, preparing for the jubilee of the year 2000. He later stated in *Tertio Millennio Adveniente,* "In fact, preparing for the *Year 2000 has become as it were a hermeneutical key of my Pontificate*" (no. 23).

During his long pontificate, he developed the teachings of Vatican II in his fourteen encyclicals and countless other writings. The collection of his teachings known as the "theology of the body" has revitalized Catholic teaching, especially in the area of marriage and the family. He inspired young people through the World Youth Days that he inaugurated and by his constant encouragement. John Paul also made great efforts in the field of ecumenism. He desired the unity of East and West, hoping that the Church would breathe with both lungs, as he put it. He also promoted efforts to foster a greater understanding between the Catholic Church and the Jewish people.

John Paul was a great Marian pope. His personal devotion to Mary had taken root in him from his earliest years. As a young man working in a chemical plant, he would carry a copy of Saint Louis de Montfort's *True Devotion to Mary* and read it in his spare time. His motto, *Totus tuus*—I am all yours—reflects his consecration to Mary. During his papacy he wrote a major Marian encyclical, *Mother of the Redeemer*, and instituted the luminous mysteries of the Rosary.

Perhaps John Paul's greatest witness was the one he gave in the last years of his life, as his health declined due to the effects of Parkinson's disease. As he lay dying the world kept vigil with him, until the Lord came for him on April 2, 2005, the evening before Divine Mercy Sunday. The great crowds that flocked to Rome to pay him homage gave a beautiful testimony to the love that he received because he had first loved us so much.

In *Crossing the Threshold of Hope*, John Paul made this remarkable statement: *"Original sin attempts . . . to abolish fatherhood,* destroying its rays which permeate the created world, placing in doubt the truth about God who is Love and leaving man only with a sense of the master-slave relationship." With this observation he was diagnosing the spiritual ills of the modern world. Original sin, and all sin after that, tries to do away with the fatherhood of God. Sin deceives us into thinking that God is a severe taskmaster, that we are nothing but slaves. We think that if we enter into a relationship with him we will end up being hoodwinked. Can we really trust God? If I turn my life over to the Lord, will I somehow end up losing my freedom? These questions haunt people today.

John Paul was very aware of this, and much of his life and papacy can be seen in the light of those important questions. He had explored this theme in a play he wrote as a young man, *The Radiation of Fatherhood.* In his philosophical work at Lublin, he had studied in depth the question of human freedom. What makes human persons unique? How do our actions make us more free, or less? Love brings us happiness, but what is authentic love? Can we evade our responsibilities in love and still find freedom and happiness?

As a pastor, he had a keen understanding not only of human sin and frailty, but also of the greatness of our call to love God and neighbor. He preached Jesus Christ, the Redeemer of the human race, as our way back to our loving Father. John Paul often urged people not to be afraid of God, because he is a Father full of merciful love, always ready to forgive. The Pope stressed divine mercy because he saw it as his mission from God. On November 22, 1981, at the Shrine of Merciful Love in Collevalenza, Italy—his first public visitation after being shot—Pope John Paul II stated, "A year ago I published the encyclical *Dives in Misericordia*. This made me come to the Sanctuary of Merciful Love today. By my presence I wish to reconfirm, in a way, the message of that encyclical. I wish to read it again and deliver it again. Right from the beginning of my ministry in Saint Peter's See in Rome, I considered this message my special task. Providence has assigned it to me in the present situation of man, the Church, and the world. It could be said that precisely this situation assigned that message to me as my task before God." Later he canonized Saint Faustina, the apostle of Divine Mercy, and established Divine Mercy Sunday as a liturgical celebration for the universal Church.

In his encyclical on the Eucharist, *Ecclesia de Eucharistia,* he summarizes the program for his pontificate: "To contemplate the face of Christ, and to contemplate it with Mary, is the 'program' which I have set before the Church at the dawn of the third millennium, summoning her to put out into the deep on the sea of history with the enthusiasm of the new evangelization" (no. 6). If original sin had sought to abolish fatherhood, Mary's fiat did just the opposite as she gave birth to the Savior, Jesus Christ.

During his long pontificate John Paul produced a vast amount of writings. The excerpts in this book were chosen to reflect some of these great themes: the mystery of human sin, the challenge to return to God with love, to find the face of the Father reflected on the face of Jesus Christ. I believe that in his own way, John Paul strove to show to the world a true spiritual fatherhood. He was intensely interested in people, and the time he took to speak to others when meeting them would often frustrate the papal "handlers" who tried to keep him on schedule. When he died, the spontaneous outpouring of affection, the millions of mourners who crowded the streets of Rome, gave eloquent testimony to the love of his great heart, the heart of a shepherd who still urges us today, "Do not be afraid! Open wide the doors to Christ!"

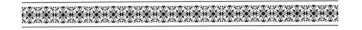

I

God the Father Seeks Us

In Jesus Christ God not only speaks to man but also *seeks him out.* The Incarnation of the Son of God attests that God goes in search of man. Jesus speaks of this search as the finding of a lost sheep (cf. Lk 15:1–7). It is a search which *begins in the heart of God* and culminates in the Incarnation of the Word. If God goes in search of man, created in his own image and likeness, he does so because he loves him eternally in the Word, and wishes to raise him in Christ to the dignity of an adoptive son. God therefore goes in search of man who *is his special possession* in a way unlike any other creature. Man is God's possession by virtue of a choice made in love: God seeks man out, moved by his fatherly heart.

Why does God seek man out? Because man has turned away from him, hiding himself as Adam did among the trees of the Garden of Eden (cf. Gen 3:8–10). *Man allowed himself to be led astray* by the enemy of God (cf. Gen 3:13). Satan deceived man, persuading him that he too was a god, that he, like God, was capable of knowing good and evil, ruling the world according to his own will without having to take into account the divine will (cf. Gen 3:5). Going in search of man through his Son, God wishes to persuade man to abandon the paths of evil which lead him farther and farther afield. "Making him abandon" those paths means making man understand that he is taking the wrong path; it means *overcoming the evil* which is everywhere found in human history. *Overcoming evil: this is the meaning of the Redemption.* This is brought about in the sacrifice of Christ, by which man redeems the debt of sin and is reconciled to God. The Son of God became man, taking a body and soul in the womb of the Virgin, precisely for this reason: to become the perfect redeeming sacrifice. The religion of the Incarnation is the *religion* of the world's *Redemption* through the sacrifice of Christ, wherein lies victory over evil, over sin, and over death itself. Accepting death on the Cross, Christ at the same time reveals and gives life, because he rises again and death no longer has power over him.

The religion which originates in the mystery of the Redemptive Incarnation is the religion of *"dwelling in the heart of God,"* of sharing in God's very life. Saint Paul speaks of this in the passage already quoted: "God has sent the Spirit of his Son into our hearts, crying, 'Abba! Father!'" (Gal 4:6). Man cries out like Christ himself, who turned to God "with loud cries and tears" (Heb 5:7), especially in Gethsemane and on the Cross; man cries out to God just as Christ cried out to him, and thus he bears witness that he shares in Christ's sonship through the power of the Holy Spirit. The Holy Spirit, whom the Father has sent in the name of the Son, enables man to share in the inmost life of God. He also enables man *to be a son, in the likeness of Christ,* and an heir of all that belongs to the Son (cf. Gal 4:7). In this consists the religion of "dwelling in the inmost life of God," which begins with the Incarnation of the Son of God. The Holy Spirit, who searches the depths of God (cf. 1 Cor 2:10), leads us, all mankind, into these depths by virtue of the sacrifice of Christ.

— Excerpt from Apostolic Letter *Tertio Millennio Adveniente*, nos. 7–8, November 10, 1994

II

The Mystery of Original Sin

According to the witness of the beginning, God in creation has revealed himself as omnipotence, which is love. At the same time he has revealed to man that, as the "image and likeness" of his Creator, he is *called to participate in truth and love*. This participation means a life in union with God, who is "eternal life."[1] But man, under the influence of the "father of lies," has separated himself from this participation. To what degree? Certainly not to the degree of the sin of a pure spirit, to the degree of the sin of Satan. The human spirit is incapable of reaching such a degree.[2] In the very description given in Genesis *it is easy to see the difference of degree* between the "breath of evil" on the part of the one who "has sinned (or remains in sin) from the beginning" (1 Jn 3:8) and already "has been judged" (Jn 16:11), and the evil of disobedience on the part of man.

Man's disobedience, nevertheless, always means a *turning away from God,* and in a certain sense *the closing up* of human freedom in his regard. It also means a certain opening of this freedom—of the human mind and will— to the one who is the "father of lies." This act of conscious choice is not only "disobedience" but also involves a *certain consent to the motivation* which was contained in the first temptation to sin and which is unceasingly renewed during the whole history of man on earth: "For God knows that when you eat of it your eyes will be opened, and you will be like God, knowing good and evil."

Here we find ourselves at the very center of what could be called the "anti-Word," that is to say the "anti-truth": For *the truth about man* becomes *falsified: who man is* and what are *the impassable limits* of his being and freedom. This "anti-truth" is possible because at the same time there is a complete *falsification* of the *truth about who God is.* God the Creator is placed in a state of suspicion, indeed of accusation, in the mind of the creature. For the first time in human history there appears the perverse "genius of suspicion." He seeks to *"falsify" Good itself; the absolute Good,* which precisely in the work of creation has manifested itself as the Good which gives in an inexpressible way: as *bonum diffusivum sui,* as *creative love.* Who can completely *"convince* concerning sin," or concerning this motivation of man's original disobedience, except the one who alone is the gift and the source of all giving of gifts, except the Spirit, who "searches the depths of God" and is the love of the Father and the Son?

For in spite of all the witness of creation and of the salvific economy inherent in it, the spirit of darkness (cf. Eph 6:12; Lk 22:53) is capable of showing *God as an enemy* of his own creature, and in the first place as an enemy of man, *as a source of danger and threat to man.* In this way *Satan* manages to sow in man's soul the seed of opposition to the one who "from the beginning" would be considered as man's enemy—and not as Father. Man is challenged to become the adversary of God!

The analysis of sin in its original dimension indicates that, through the influence of the "father of lies," *throughout the history of humanity there will be a constant pressure on man to reject God,* even to the point of hating him: *"Love of self to the point of contempt for God,"* as Saint Augustine puts it.[3] Man will be inclined to see in God primarily a limitation of himself, and not the source of his own freedom and the fullness of good. We see this confirmed in the modern age, when the atheistic ideologies seek *to root out religion* on the grounds that religion causes the radical *"alienation" of man,* as if man were dispossessed of his own humanity when, accepting the idea of God, he attributes to God what belongs to man, and exclusively to man! Hence a process of thought and historico-sociological practice in which the rejection of God has reached the point of declaring his "death." An absurdity, both in concept and expression! But the ideology of the "death of God" is more a threat to *man,* as the Second Vatican Council indicates when it analyzes the question of the "independence of earthly affairs" and writes: "For without the Creator the creature would disappear . . . when God is forgotten the creature itself grows unintelligible."[4] The ideology of the "death of God" easily demonstrates in its effects that on the "theoretical and practical" levels it is the ideology of the "death of man."

— Excerpt from Encyclical Letter
Dominum et Vivificantem, nos. 37–38, May 18, 1986

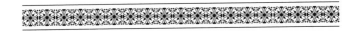

III

The Love of God the Father

The Apostle John urges us: "Beloved, let us love one another; for love is of God, and he who loves is born of God and knows God. He who does not love does not know God; for God is love" (1 Jn 4:7–8).

While these sublime words reveal to us the very essence of God as a mystery of infinite charity, they also lay the basis for the Christian moral life, which is summed up in the commandment of love.

The human person is called to love God with total commitment and to relate to his brothers and sisters with a loving attitude inspired by God's own love. Conversion means being converted to love.

In the Old Testament the inner dynamics of this commandment can already be seen in the covenant relationship established by God with Israel: on the one hand, there is the initiative of God's love, and, on the other, the response of love that he expects from Israel. This is how, for example, the divine initiative is presented in the Book of Deuteronomy: "It was not because you were more in number than any other people that the LORD set his love upon you and chose you, for you were the fewest of all peoples; but it is because the LORD loves you" (Dt 7:7–8). The basic commandment that directs Israel's entire religious life corresponds to this preferential, totally gratuitous love: "You shall love the LORD your God with all your heart, and with all your soul, and with all your might" (Dt 6:5).

The loving God is a God who is not remote, but intervenes in history. When he reveals his name to Moses, he does so to assure him of his loving assistance in the saving event of the Exodus, an assistance which will last for ever (cf. Ex 3:15). Through the prophets' words, he would continually remind his people of this act of love. We read, for example, in Jeremiah: "Thus says the LORD: 'The people who survived the sword found grace in the wilderness; when Israel sought for rest, the LORD appeared to him from afar. I have loved you with an everlasting love; therefore I have continued my faithfulness to you'" (Jer 31:2–3).

It is a love which takes on tones of immense tenderness (cf. Hos 11:8f.; Jer 31:20) and normally uses the image of a father, but sometimes is also expressed in a spousal metaphor: "I will betroth you to me for ever; I will betroth you to me in righteousness and in justice, in steadfast love and in mercy" (Hos 2:19; cf. vv. 18–25).

Even after seeing his people's repeated unfaithfulness to the covenant, this God is still willing to offer his love, creating in man a new heart that enables him to accept the law he is given without reserve, as we read in the prophet Jeremiah: "I will put my law within them, and I will write it upon their hearts" (Jer 31:33). Likewise in Ezekiel we read: "A new heart I will give you, and a new spirit I will put within you; and I will take out of your flesh the heart of stone and give you a heart of flesh" (Ez 36:26).

In the New Testament this dynamic of love is centered on Jesus, the Father's beloved Son (cf. Jn 3:35; 5:20; 10:17), who reveals himself through him. Men and women share in this love by knowing the Son, that is, by accepting his teaching and his work of redemption.

We can only come to the Father's love by imitating the Son in his keeping of the Father's commandments: "As the Father has loved me, so have I loved you; abide in my love.

If you keep my commandments, you will abide in my love, just as I have kept my Father's commandments and abide in his love" (Jn 15:9–10). In this way we also come to share in the Son's knowledge of the Father: "No longer do I call you servants, for the servant does not know what his master is doing; but I have called you friends, for all that I have heard from my Father I have made known to you" (Jn 15:15). . . .

The Paraclete is the One through whom we experience God's fatherly love. Moreover, the most comforting effect of his presence in us is precisely the certainty that this eternal and boundless love with which God loved us first will never abandon us: "Who shall separate us from the love of Christ? . . . For I am sure that neither death, nor life, nor angels, nor principalities, nor things present, nor things to come, nor powers, nor height, nor depth, nor anything else in all creation, will be able to separate us from the love of God in Christ Jesus our Lord" (Rom 8:35, 38–39). The new heart, which loves and knows, beats in harmony with God who loves with an everlasting love.

— Excerpt from General Audience of October 6, 1999

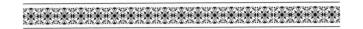

IV

Divine Mercy

"Give thanks to the LORD for he is good; his steadfast love endures for ever" (Ps 118:1). So the Church sings on the Octave of Easter, as if receiving from Christ's lips these words of the Psalm; from the lips of the risen Christ, who bears the great message of divine mercy and entrusts its ministry to the Apostles in the Upper Room: "Peace be with you. As the Father has sent me, even so I send you. . . . Receive the Holy Spirit. If you forgive the sins of any, they are forgiven; if you retain the sins of any, they are retained" (Jn 20:21–23).

Before speaking these words, Jesus shows his hands and his side. He points, that is, to the wounds of the

Passion, especially the wound in his heart, the source from which flows the great wave of mercy poured out on humanity. From that heart Sister Faustina Kowalska, the blessed whom from now on we will call a saint, will see two rays of light shining from that heart and illuminating the world: *"The two rays,"* Jesus himself explained to her one day, *"represent blood and water."*[1]

Blood and water! We immediately think of the testimony given by the Evangelist John, who, when a solider on Calvary pierced Christ's side with his spear, sees blood and water flowing from it (cf. Jn 19:34). Moreover, if the blood recalls the sacrifice of the Cross and the gift of the Eucharist, the water, in Johannine symbolism, represents not only Baptism but also the gift of the Holy Spirit (cf. Jn 3:5; 4:14; 7:37–39).

Divine Mercy reaches human beings through the heart of Christ crucified: *"My daughter, say that I am love and mercy personified,"* Jesus will ask Sister Faustina.[2] Christ pours out this mercy on humanity though the sending of the Spirit who, in the Trinity, is the Person-Love. And is not mercy love's "second name"[3] understood in its deepest and most tender aspect, in its ability to take upon itself the burden of any need and, especially, in its immense capacity for forgiveness?

What will the years ahead bring us? What will man's future on earth be like? We are not given to know. However, it is certain that in addition to new progress there will unfortunately be no lack of painful experiences. But the light of divine mercy, which the Lord in a way wished to return to the world through Sister Faustina's charism, will illumine the way for the men and women of the third millennium.

However, as the Apostles once did, today too humanity must welcome into the upper room of history the risen Christ, who shows the wounds of his Crucifixion and repeats: *Peace be with you!* Humanity must let itself be touched and pervaded by the Spirit given to it by the risen Christ. It is the Spirit who heals the wounds of the heart, pulls down the barriers that separate us from God and divide us from one another, and, at the same time, restores the joy of the Father's love and of fraternal unity.

It is important then that we accept the whole message that comes to us from the word of God on this Second Sunday of Easter, which from now on throughout the Church *will be called "Divine Mercy Sunday."* In the various readings, the liturgy seems to indicate the path of mercy which, while re-establishing the relationship of each person with God, also creates new relations of fraternal solidarity among human beings. Christ has taught us that "man not only receives and experiences the mercy of God, but is also called 'to practice mercy' toward others: 'Blessed are the merciful, for they shall obtain mercy' (Mt 5:7)."[4]

He also showed us the many paths of mercy, which not only forgives sins but reaches out to all human needs. Jesus bent over every kind of human poverty, material and spiritual. . . .

Sister Faustina's canonization has a particular eloquence: by this act I intend today to pass this message on to the new millennium. I pass it on to all people, so that they will learn to know ever better the true face of God and the true face of their brethren.

In fact, love of God and love of one's brothers and sisters are inseparable, as the First Letter of John has reminded us: "By this we know that we love the children of God, when we love God and obey his commandments" (5:2). Here the Apostle reminds us of the truth of love, showing us its measure and criterion in the observance of the commandments.

It is not easy to love with a deep love, which lies in the authentic gift of self. This love can only be learned by penetrating the mystery of God's love. Looking at him, being one with his fatherly heart, we are able to look with new eyes at our brothers and sisters, with an attitude of unselfishness and solidarity, of generosity and forgiveness. All this is mercy! . . .

[T]he message of divine mercy is also implicitly *a message about the value of every human being.* Each person is precious in God's eyes; Christ gave his life for each one; to everyone the Father gives his Spirit and offers intimacy.

This consoling message is addressed above all to those who, afflicted by a particularly harsh trial or crushed by the weight of the sins they committed, have lost all confidence in life and are tempted to give in to despair. To them the gentle face of Christ is offered; those rays from his heart touch them and shine upon them, warm them, show them the way, and fill them with hope. How many souls have been consoled by the prayer *"Jesus, I trust in you,"* which Providence intimated through Sister Faustina! This simple act of abandonment to Jesus dispels the thickest clouds and lets a ray of light penetrate every life.

— Excerpt from homily given in Saint Peter's Square for the canonization of Saint Mary Faustina Kowalska, April 30, 2000

V

Christ and the Mystery of Redemption

Jesus Christ, the Son of the living God, become our reconciliation with the Father (Rom 5:11; Col 1:20). He it was, and he alone, who satisfied the Father's eternal love, that fatherhood which from the beginning found expression in creating the world, giving man all the riches of creation, and making him "little less than God" (Ps 8:6), in that he was created "in the image and after the likeness of God" (cf. Gen 1:26). He and he alone also satisfied that fatherhood of God and that love which man in a way rejected by breaking the first Covenant (cf. Gen 3:6–13) and the later covenants that God "again and again offered to man."[1] The redemption of the world—this tremendous mystery of love in which creation is renewed[2]—is, at its deepest root, the fullness of justice in a human Heart—the Heart of the Firstborn Son—in order that it may become justice in the hearts of many human beings, predestined from eternity in the Firstborn Son to be children of God (cf. Rom 8:29–30; Eph 1:8) and called to grace, called to love. The Cross on Calvary, through which Jesus Christ—a Man, the Son of the Virgin Mary, thought to be the son of Joseph of Nazareth—"leaves" this world, is also a fresh manifestation of the eternal fatherhood of God, who in him draws near again to humanity, to each human being, giving him the thrice holy "Spirit of truth" (cf. Jn 16:13).

This revelation of the Father and outpouring of the Holy Spirit, which stamp an indelible seal on the mystery of the Redemption, explain the meaning of the Cross and death of Christ. The God of creation is revealed as the God of redemption, as the God who is "faithful to himself" (cf. 1 Thess 5:24), and faithful to his love for man and the world, which he revealed on the day of creation. His is a love that does not draw back before anything that justice requires in him. Therefore "for our sake [God] made him [the Son] to be sin who knew no sin" (2 Cor 5:21; cf. Gal 3:13). If he "made to be sin" him who was without any sin whatever, it was to reveal the love that is always greater than the whole of creation, the love that is he himself, since "God is love" (1 Jn 4:8, 16). Above all, love is greater than sin, than weakness, than the "futility of creation" (cf. Rom 8:20), it is stronger than death; it is a love always ready to raise up and forgive, always ready to go to meet the prodigal son (cf. Lk 15:11–32), always looking for "the revealing of the sons of God" (Rom 8:19), who are called to the glory that is to be revealed" (Rom 8:18). This revelation of love is also described as mercy;[3] and in man's history this revelation of love and mercy has taken a form and a name: that of Jesus Christ.

— Excerpt from Encyclical Letter *Redemptor Hominis*,
no. 9, March 4, 1979

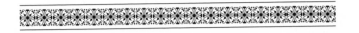

VI

Believing in the Crucified Son Means Seeing the Father

The Cross on Calvary, the Cross upon which Christ conducts his final dialogue with the Father, *emerges from the very heart of the love* that man, created in the image and likeness of God, has been given as a gift, according to God's eternal plan. God, as Christ has revealed him, does not merely remain closely linked with the world as the Creator and the ultimate source of existence. He is also Father: he is linked to man, whom he called to existence in the visible world, by a bond still more intimate than that of creation. It is love which not only creates the good but also grants participation in the very life of God: Father,

Son, and Holy Spirit. For he who loves desires to give himself.

The Cross of Christ on Calvary stands *beside the path of that admirable commercium*, of that *wonderful self-communication of God to man*, which also includes the call to man to share in the divine life by giving himself, and with himself the whole visible world, to God, and like an adopted son to become a sharer in the truth and love which is in God and proceeds from God. It is precisely beside the path of man's eternal election to the dignity of being an adopted child of God that there stands in history the Cross of Christ, the only-begotten Son, who, as "light from light, true God from true God,"[1] came to give the final witness to the wonderful *covenant of God with humanity, of God with man*—every human being. This covenant, as old as man—it goes back to the very mystery of creation—and afterward many times renewed with one single chosen people, is equally the new and definitive covenant, which was established there on Calvary, and is not limited to a single people, to Israel, but is open to each and every individual.

What else, then, does the Cross of Christ say to us, the Cross that in a sense is the final word of his messianic message and mission? And yet this is not yet the word of the God of the covenant: that will be pronounced at the dawn when first the women and then the Apostles come to the tomb of the crucified Christ, see the tomb empty, and for the first time hear the message: "He is risen." They will repeat this message to the others and will be witnesses to the risen Christ. Yet, even in this glorification of the Son of God, the Cross remains, that Cross which—through all the messianic testimony of the Man the Son, who suffered death upon it—*speaks and never ceases to speak of God the Father, who is absolutely faithful to his eternal love for man*, since he "so loved the world"—therefore man in the world—that "he gave his only Son, that whoever believes in him should not perish but have eternal life" (Jn 3:16). Believing in the crucified Son means "seeing the Father" (cf. Jn 14:9), means believing that love is present in the world and that this love is more powerful than any kind of evil in which individuals, humanity, or the world are involved. Believing in this love means *believing in mercy*. For mercy is an indispensable dimension of love; it is as it were love's second name and, at the same time, the specific manner in which love is revealed and effected vis-à-vis the reality of the evil that is in the world, affecting and besieging man, insinuating itself even into his heart and capable of causing him to "perish in Gehenna" (Mt 10:28).

— Excerpt from Encyclical Letter *Dives in Misericordia*, no. 7, November 30, 1980

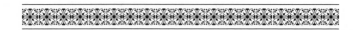

VII

The Compassion of the Father

More often the Sacred Book speaks to us of a Father who feels compassion for man, as though sharing his pain. In a word, this inscrutable and indescribable *fatherly "pain" will bring about* above all the *wonderful economy of redemptive love* in Jesus Christ, so that through the *mysterium pietatis* love can reveal itself in the history of man as stronger than sin. So that the "gift" may prevail!

The Holy Spirit, who in the words of Jesus "convinces concerning sin," is the love of the Father and the Son, and as such is the Trinitarian gift, and at the same time the eternal source of every divine giving of gifts to creatures. Precisely in him we can picture as personified and actualized in a transcendent way that mercy which the patristic and theological tradition, following the line of the Old and New Testaments, attributes to God. In man, mercy includes sorrow and compassion for the misfortunes of one's neighbor. In God, the Spirit-Love expresses the consideration of human sin in a fresh outpouring of salvific love. From God, in the unity of the Father with the Son, the economy of salvation is born, the economy which fills the history of man with the gifts of the Redemption. Whereas sin, by rejecting love, has caused the "suffering" of man which in some way has affected the whole of creation (cf. Rom 8:20–22), *the Holy Spirit* will enter into human and cosmic suffering with a new outpouring of love, which will redeem the world. And on the lips of Jesus the Redeemer, in whose humanity the "suffering" of God is concretized, there will be heard a word which manifests the eternal love full of mercy: *"Misereor"* (cf. Mt 15:32; Mk 8:2). Thus, on the part of the Holy Spirit, "convincing of sin" becomes a manifestation before creation, which is "subjected to futility," and above all in the depth of human consciences, that *sin is conquered through the sacrifice of the Lamb of God* who has become even "unto death" *the obedient servant* who, by making up for man's *disobedience*, accomplishes the redemption of the world. In this way the spirit of truth, the Paraclete, "convinces concerning sin."

— Excerpt from Encyclical Letter *Dominum et Vivificantem*, no. 39, May 18, 1986

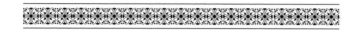

VIII

The Holy Spirit Brings Us to Conversion

The words of the Risen Christ on the "first day of the week" *give particular emphasis to the presence of the Paraclete-Counselor* as the one who "convinces the world concerning sin, righteousness, and judgment." For it is only in this relationship that it is possible to explain the words which Jesus directly relates to the "gift" of the Holy Spirit to the Apostles. He says: "Receive the Holy Spirit. If you forgive the sins of any, they are forgiven; if you retain the sins of any, they are retained" (Jn 20:22–23). Jesus confers on the Apostles the power to forgive sins, so that they may pass it on to their successors in the Church. But this power granted to men presupposes and includes the saving action of the Holy Spirit. By becoming "the light of hearts,"[1] that is to say the light of consciences, the Holy Spirit "convinces concerning sin," which is to say, he *makes man realize his own evil* and at the same time *directs him toward what is good.* Thanks to the multiplicity of the Spirit's gifts, by reason of which he is invoked as the "sevenfold one," every kind of human sin can be reached by God's saving power. In reality—as Saint Bonaventure says—"by virtue of the seven gifts of the Holy Spirit all evils are destroyed and all good things are produced."[2]

Thus *the conversion of the human heart,* which is an indispensable condition for the forgiveness of sins, is brought about by the influence of the Counselor. Without a true conversion, which implies inner contrition, and without a sincere and firm purpose of amendment, sins remain "unforgiven," in the words of Jesus, and with him in the Tradition of the Old and New Covenants. For the first words uttered by Jesus at the beginning of his ministry, according to the *Gospel of Mark*, are these: "Repent, and believe in the Gospel" (Mk 1:15). A confirmation of this exhortation is the "convincing concerning sin" that the Holy Spirit undertakes in a new way by virtue of the Redemption accomplished by the Blood of the Son of Man. Hence the *Letter to the Hebrews* says that this "blood purifies the conscience" (cf. Heb 9:14). It therefore, so to speak, *opens to the Holy Spirit* the door into man's inmost being, namely into the sanctuary of human consciences.

— Excerpt from Encyclical Letter *Dominum et Vivificantem*, no. 42, May 18, 1986

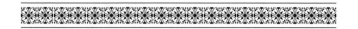

IX

The Eucharist

Let us now turn our gaze to the Gospel account of the *multiplication of the loaves,* which completes the Eucharistic triptych brought to our attention today. In the liturgical setting of *Corpus Christi,* this passage from the Evangelist Luke helps us to understand better the gift and mystery of the Eucharist.

Jesus took the five loaves and the two fish, raised his eyes to heaven, blessed them, broke them, and gave them to the Apostles to distribute to the crowd (cf. Lk 9:16). "All," Saint Luke remarks, "ate and were satisfied. And they took up what was left over, twelve baskets of broken pieces" (cf. Lk 9:17).

This is an amazing miracle which marks in a way *the beginning of a long historical process*: the uninterrupted multiplication in the Church of the Bread of new life for the people of every race and culture. This sacramental ministry is entrusted to the Apostles and to their successors. And they, faithful to the divine Master's command, never cease to break and distribute the Eucharistic bread from generation to generation.

The People of God receive it with devout participation. With this Bread of life, a remedy of immortality, countless saints and martyrs were nourished and from it drew the strength to resist even harsh and prolonged sufferings. They believed in the words that Jesus once spoke in Capernaum: "I myself am the living bread come down from heaven. If any one eats this bread, he will live forever" (Jn 6:51).

After contemplating the extraordinary Eucharistic "triptych" made up of today's readings, let us now turn our mind's eye directly to the mystery. Jesus calls himself "the Bread of life," adding: "The bread I will give is my flesh, for the life of the world" (Jn 6:51).

The mystery of our salvation! Christ—*the only Lord yesterday, today, and for ever*—wanted his saving presence in the world and in history to be linked with *the sacrament of the Eucharist*. He wanted to make himself the bread which is broken so that everyone can be nourished by his very life through participation in the sacrament of his Body and Blood.

Like the disciples who listened in astonishment to his discourse at Capernaum, we also find this language hard to understand (cf. Jn 6:60). We might sometimes be tempted to give it a reductive interpretation. But this would take us far from Christ, as was the case with those disciples who "after that no longer went about with him" (Jn 6:66).

We would like to stay with Christ and for this reason we say to him with Peter: "Lord, to whom shall we go? You have the words of eternal life" (Jn 6:68). With the same conviction as Peter, let us kneel today before the sacrament of the altar and renew our profession of faith in the real presence of Christ.

This is the meaning of today's celebration, which is given special emphasis by the International Eucharistic Congress in the year of the Great Jubilee. This is also the sense of the solemn procession which, as it does every year, will shortly make its way from this square to the Basilica of Saint Mary Major.

With humble pride we will escort the Eucharistic Sacrament through the streets of the city, close by the buildings where people live, rejoice, and suffer; between the shops and offices where they work each day. We will bring it into contact with our lives beset by a thousand dangers, weighed down by worries and sorrows, subject to the slow but inexorable wear and tear of time.

As we escort him, we will offer him the tribute of our hymns and prayers: *"Bone Pastor, panis vere. . . . True Bread, Good Shepherd, tend us,"* we will say to him with trust, *"Jesus, of your love befriend us, / You refresh us, you defend us, / Your eternal goodness send us. You who all things can and know, / Who on earth such food bestow, / Grant us with your saints, though lowest, / Where the heavenly feast you show, / Fellow heirs and guests to be."*

Amen!

— Excerpt from homily given for feast of Corpus Christi,
June 22, 2000

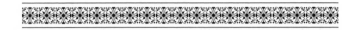

X

To Young People

The Spirit awakens the desire for truth in every heart. The truth which sets us free is Christ, the only one who can say: "I am the truth" (Jn 14:6), and adds: "If you continue in my word, you are truly my disciples, and you will know the truth, and the truth will make you free" (Jn 8:31–32).

Many of you are studying, others are already working or looking for a job. It is important that you all become impassioned seekers of the truth and its fearless witnesses. Never resign yourselves to lies, falsehood, or compromise! React strongly to those who attempt to ensnare your intelligence and lure your heart with messages and suggestions that make you slaves of consumerism, disordered sex and violence, to the point of being driven into the void of loneliness and the meanders of the culture of death. Detached from truth, every freedom becomes a new and more burdensome slavery.

Free to love! Dear young people, who does not want to love and to be loved? But to experience sincere love, you must open the door of your heart to Jesus and take the way he marked out with his own life: the way of self-giving. This is the secret to the success of any real call to love, particularly of that call born in a surprising way in an adolescent's heart which leads to marriage, the priesthood, or the consecrated life.

When a young man or woman recognizes that authentic love is a precious treasure, they are also enabled to live their sexuality in accordance with the divine plan, rejecting the false models which are, unfortunately, all too frequently publicized and very widespread.

Of course, it is a demanding choice; but it is the only one that really makes us free and happy, because it fulfills the deep desire the Lord has instilled in every man and woman's inmost heart.

True freedom is found where Christ's Spirit dwells (cf. 2 Cor 3:17): this is the eternal youth of the Gospel that renews persons, cultures, and the world.

Free to serve! Service, especially to the poorest and the most marginalized, is one of the vocations that appeals most to your hearts.

The Gospel passage guiding our reflection tells of a hungry crowd: Jesus takes care of them. In our city too there are people who hunger for material food and perhaps, even more, for spiritual sustenance.

During my pastoral visits to parishes, the young and the old, families and immigrants often point out to me situations of social hardship, loneliness, and neglect. So much material and spiritual poverty exists. Difficulties and problems are also visibly affecting the world of youth.

Jesus asks us not to lose heart and to fight against any form of degradation; he asks us to be fully committed to creating a civilization with a human face. As the examples of many holy people past and present show, it is already possible to weave a web of authentic relationships between people by loving and fostering life, by working constantly to ensure that every person is recognized as a child of God who is welcomed with love, whose growth is supported and whose rights are protected.

Life raises many questions, but one above all must be answered: *What sense is there in living and what awaits us after death?* This is a question which gives meaning to all existence. Perhaps some of your peers no longer wonder about it: they live in the present as if that were the whole of life. They passively abandon themselves to reality as if it were a vanishing dream, rather than strive to make values and lofty ideals more and more a reality.

Opening the door to Christ the Savior means once again to set high goals in life. Do not be satisfied with commonplace experiences; give no credit to those who offer them to you. Have faith in life and open your hearts to Christ, the Life that overcomes death!

The risen Jesus becomes our food in the Eucharist and from that point introduces us into immortal life, guaranteeing that one day we will be able to achieve it to the full and for ever. This certitude gives us the courage to face every hardship and make life a gift without reserve for God and our neighbor. This is an extraordinary adventure; but we cannot bring it to conclusion by ourselves. This is why Jesus wanted the Church, his Mystical Body and the People of the New Covenant.

— Excerpt from a Letter to the Young People of Rome,
September 8, 1997

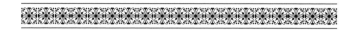

XI

The Importance of Families

In this Letter I wish to speak not to families "in the abstract" but *to every particular family in every part of the world,* wherever it is located and whatever the diversity and complexity of its culture and history. The love with which God "loved the world" (Jn 3:16), the love with which Christ loved each and every one "to the end" (Jn 13:1), makes it possible to address this message to each family, as a living "cell" of the great and universal "family" of mankind. The Father, Creator of the universe, and the Word Incarnate, the Redeemer of humanity, are the source of this universal openness to all people as brothers and sisters, and they impel us *to embrace them in the prayer* which begins with the tender words: *"Our Father."*

Prayer makes the Son of God present among us: "For where two or three are gathered in my name, I am there among them" (Mt 18:20). This *Letter to Families* wishes in the first place to be a prayer to Christ to remain in every human family; an invitation to him, in and through the small family of parents and children, to dwell in the great family of nations, so that together with him all of us can truly say: "Our Father"! Prayer must become the dominant element of the Year of the Family in the Church: prayer by the family, prayer for the family, and prayer with the family.

It is significant that precisely *in and through prayer, man comes to discover in a very simple and yet profound way his own unique subjectivity*: in prayer the human "I" more easily perceives the depth of what it means to be a person. *This is also true of the family*, which is not only the basic "cell" of society, but also possesses a particular subjectivity of its own. This subjectivity finds its first and fundamental confirmation, and is strengthened, precisely when the members of the family meet in the common invocation: "Our Father." Prayer increases the strength and spiritual unity of the family, helping the family to partake of God's own "strength." In the solemn nuptial blessing during the rite of marriage, the celebrant calls upon the Lord in these words: "Pour out upon them the grace of the Holy Spirit so that by your love poured into their hearts they will remain faithful in the marriage covenant." This "visitation" of the Holy Spirit gives rise to the inner strength of families, as well as the power capable of uniting them in love and truth.

— Excerpt from the *Letter to Families*, no. 4,
February 2, 1994

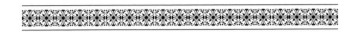

XII

The Human Person
Is the Image of God

The universe, immense and diverse as it is, the world of all living beings, *is inscribed in God's fatherhood, which is its source* (cf. Eph 3:14–16). This can be said, of course, on the basis of an analogy, thanks to which we can discern, at the very beginning of the Book of Genesis, the reality of fatherhood and motherhood and consequently of the human family. The interpretative key enabling this discernment is provided by the principle of the "image" and "likeness" of God highlighted by the scriptural text (Gen 1:26). God creates by the power of his word: "Let there be . . . !" (e.g., Gen 1:3). Significantly, in the creation of man this word of God is followed by these other words: *"Let us make man* in our image, after our likeness" (Gen 1:26). Before creating man, the Creator withdraws as it were into himself, in order to seek the pattern and inspiration in the mystery of his Being, which is already here disclosed as the divine "We." From this mystery the human being comes forth by an act of creation: *"God created man in his own image*, in the image of God he created him; male and female he created them" (Gen 1:27).

God speaks to these newly-created beings and he blesses them: "Be fruitful and multiply, and fill the earth and subdue it" (Gen 1:28). The Book of Genesis employs the same expressions used earlier for the creation of other living beings: "multiply." But it is clear that these expressions are being used in an analogous sense. Is there not present here the analogy of begetting and of fatherhood and motherhood, which should be understood in the light of the overall context? No living being on earth except man was created "in the image and likeness of God." Human fatherhood and motherhood, while remaining *biologically similar* to that of other living beings in nature, contain in an essential and unique way a *"likeness" to God* which is the basis of the family as a community of human life, as a community of persons united in love (*communio personarum*).

In the light of the New Testament it is possible to discern how *the primordial model of the family is to be sought in*

God himself, in the Trinitarian mystery of his life. The divine "We" is the eternal pattern of the human "we," especially of that "we" formed by the man and the woman created in the divine image and likeness. The words of the Book of Genesis contain that truth about man which is confirmed by the very experience of humanity. Man is created "from the very beginning" as male and female: the life of all humanity—whether of small communities or of society as a whole—is marked by this primordial duality. From it there derive the "masculinity" and the "femininity" of individuals, just as from it every community draws its own unique richness in the mutual fulfillment of persons. This is what seems to be meant by the words of the Book of Genesis: "Male and female he created them" (Gen 1:27). Here too we find the first statement of the equal dignity of man and woman: both, in equal measure, are persons. Their constitution, with the specific dignity which derives from it, defines "from the beginning" the qualities of the common good of humanity, in every dimension and circumstance of life. To this common good both man and woman make their specific contribution. Hence one can discover, at the very origins of human society, the qualities of communion and of complementarity.

— Excerpt from the *Letter to Families*, no. 6, February 2, 1994

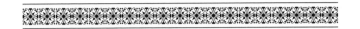

XIII

Our Restless Hearts

From the very moment of conception, and then of birth, the new being is meant *to express fully his humanity*, to "find himself" as a person. This is true for absolutely everyone, including the chronically ill and the disabled. "To be human" is his fundamental vocation: "to be human" in accordance with the gift received, in accordance with that "talent" which is humanity itself, and only then in accordance with other talents. In this sense God wills every man "for his own sake." *In God's plan*, however, the vocation of the human person extends beyond the boundaries of time. It encounters the will of the Father revealed in the Incarnate Word: *God's will is to lavish upon man a sharing in his own divine life.* As Christ says: "I came that they may have life and have it abundantly" (Jn 10:10).

Does affirming man's ultimate destiny not conflict with the statement that God wills man "for his own sake"? If he has been created for divine life, can man truly exist "for his own sake"? This is a critical question, one of great significance both for the beginning of his earthly life and its end: it is important for the whole span of his life. It might appear that in destining man for divine life, God definitively takes away man's existing "for his own sake." What then is the relationship between the life of the person and his sharing in the life of the Trinity? Saint Augustine provides us with the answer in his celebrated phrase: "Our heart is restless until it rests in you." This "restless heart" serves to point out that between the one finality and the other there is in fact no contradiction, but rather a relationship, a complementarity, a unity. By his very genealogy, the person created in the image and likeness of God *exists "for his own sake"* and reaches fulfillment precisely *by sharing in God's life.* The content of this self-fulfillment is the fullness of life in God, proclaimed by Christ (cf. Jn 6:37–40), who redeemed us precisely so that we might come to share it (cf. Mk 10:45).

It is for themselves that married couples want children; in children they see the crowning of their own love for each other. They want children for the family, as a *priceless gift.* This is quite understandable. Nonetheless, in conjugal love and in paternal and maternal love we should find inscribed the same truth about man which the Council expressed in a clear and concise way in its statement that God "willed man for his own sake." It is thus necessary that the will of the parents should be in harmony with the will of God. *They must want the new human creature in the same way as the Creator wants him:* "for himself." Our human will is always and inevitably subject to the law of time and change. The divine will, on the other hand, is eternal. As we read in the book of the prophet Jeremiah: "Before I formed you in the womb I knew you, and before you were born I consecrated you" (Jer 1:5). The genealogy of the person is thus united with the eternity of God, and only then with human fatherhood and motherhood, which are realized in time. At the moment of conception itself, man is already destined to eternity in God.

— Excerpt from the *Letter to Families*, no. 9, February 2, 1994

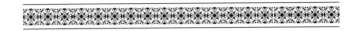

XIV

The Sincere Gift of Self

After affirming that man is the only creature on earth which God willed for itself, the Council immediately goes on to say that he cannot *"fully find himself except through a sincere gift of self."* This might appear to be a contradiction, but in fact it is not. Instead it is the magnificent paradox of human existence: an existence called *to serve the truth in love.* Love causes man to find fulfillment through the sincere gift of self. To love means to give and to receive something which can be neither bought nor sold, but only given freely and mutually.

By its very nature the gift of the person must be lasting and irrevocable. The indissolubility of marriage flows in the first place from the very essence of that gift: *the gift of one person to another person.* This reciprocal giving of self reveals the *spousal nature of love.* In their marital consent the bride and groom call each other by name: *"I . . . take you . . . as my wife (as my husband) and I promise to be true to you . . . for all the days of my life."* A gift such as this involves an obligation much more serious and profound than anything which might be "purchased" in any way and at any price. Kneeling before the Father, from whom all fatherhood and motherhood come, the future parents come to realize that they have been "redeemed." They have been purchased at great cost, *by the price* of the most sincere gift of all, *the Blood of Christ* of which they partake through the Sacrament. The liturgical crowning of the marriage rite is the Eucharist, the sacrifice of that "Body which has been given up" and that "Blood which has been shed," which in a certain way finds expression in the consent of the spouses.

When a man and woman in marriage mutually give and receive each other in the unity of "one flesh," the logic of the sincere gift of self becomes a part of their life. Without this, marriage would be empty; whereas a communion of persons, built on this logic, becomes a communion of parents. When they transmit *life to the child, a new human "thou" becomes a part of the horizon of the "we" of the spouses,* a person whom they will call by a new name: "our son . . . ; our daughter. . . ." "I have gotten a man with the help of the LORD" (Gen 4:1), says Eve, the first woman of history: a human being, first expected for nine months and then "revealed" to parents, brothers, and sisters. The process from conception and growth in the mother's womb to birth makes it possible to create a space within which the new creature can be revealed as a "gift": indeed this is what it is from the very beginning. Could this frail and helpless being, totally dependent upon its parents and completely entrusted to them, be seen in any other way? The newborn child gives itself to its parents by the very fact of its coming into existence. *Its existence is already a gift, the first gift of the Creator to the creature.*

In the newborn child is realized the common good of the family. Just as the common good of spouses is fulfilled in conjugal love, ever ready to give and receive new life, so too the common good of the family is fulfilled through that same spousal love, as embodied in the newborn child. Part of the genealogy of the person is the genealogy of the family, preserved for posterity by the annotations in the Church's baptismal registers, even though these are merely the social consequence of the fact that "a man has been born into the world" (cf. Jn 16:21).

— Excerpt from the *Letter to Families*, no. 11, February 2, 1994

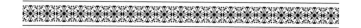

XV

We Can Count on Mary's Intercession

Down the centuries Marian devotion has enjoyed an uninterrupted development. In addition to the traditional liturgical feasts dedicated to the Lord's Mother, there has been a flowering of countless expressions of piety, often approved and encouraged by the Church's Magisterium. . . .

The first known Marian invocation goes back to the third century and begins with the words: "We fly to thy patronage (*Sub tuum praesidium*), O holy Mother of God. . . ." However, since the fourteenth century the most common prayer among Christians has been the "Hail Mary."

By repeating the first words the angel addressed to Mary, it leads the faithful to contemplate the mystery of the Incarnation. The Latin word "ave" translates the Greek word "chaïré": it is an invitation to joy and could be translated "rejoice." The Eastern hymn *"Akathistos"* repeatedly stresses this "rejoice." In the "Hail Mary" the Blessed Virgin is called "full of grace" and is thus recognized for the perfection and beauty of her soul.

The phrase "the Lord is with thee" reveals God's special personal relationship with Mary, which fits into the great plan for his covenant with all humanity. Next, the statement "blessed art thou among women and blessed is the fruit of thy womb, Jesus" expresses the fulfillment of the divine plan in the Daughter of Zion's virginal body.

Calling upon "holy Mary, Mother of God," Christians ask the one who was the immaculate Mother of the Lord by a unique privilege: "Pray for us sinners," and entrust themselves to her at the present moment and at the ultimate moment of death.

The traditional prayer of the "Angelus" also invites Christians to meditate on the mystery of the Incarnation, urging them to take Mary as their point of reference at different times of their day in order to imitate her willingness to fulfill the divine plan of salvation. This prayer makes us relive in a way that great event in human history, the Incarnation, to which every "Hail Mary" refers. Here we find the value and attraction of the "Angelus," expressed so many times not only by theologians and pastors but also by poets and painters.

In Marian devotion the Rosary has taken on an important role. By repeating the "Hail Mary," it leads us to contemplate the mysteries of faith. In nourishing the Christian people's love for the Mother of God, this simple prayer also orients Marian prayer in a clearer way to its goal: the glorification of Christ. . . .

As the liturgy and Christian piety demonstrate, the Church has always held devotion to Mary in high esteem, considering it inseparably linked to belief in Christ. It is in fact based on the Father's plan, the Savior's will, and the Paraclete's inspiration.

Having received salvation and grace from Christ, the Blessed Virgin is called to play an important role in humanity's redemption. Through Marian devotion Christians acknowledge the value of Mary's presence on their journey to salvation, having recourse to her for every kind of grace. They especially know that they can count on her motherly intercession to receive from the Lord everything necessary for growing in the divine life and for attaining eternal salvation.

As the many titles attributed to the Blessed Virgin and

the continual pilgrimages to Marian shrines attest, the trust of the faithful in Jesus's Mother spurs them to call upon her for their daily needs. They are certain that her maternal heart cannot remain indifferent to the material and spiritual distress of her children. By encouraging the confidence and spontaneity of the faithful, devotion to the Mother of God thus helps to brighten their spiritual life and enables them to make progress on the demanding path of the Beatitudes.

Lastly, we would like to recall that devotion to Mary, by highlighting the human dimension of the Incarnation, helps us better to discern the face of a God who shares the joys and sufferings of humanity, the "God-with-us" whom she conceived as man in her most pure womb, gave birth to, cared for, and followed with unspeakable love from his days in Nazareth and Bethlehem to those of the Cross and Resurrection.

— Excerpt from the General Audience of November 5, 1997

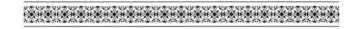

XVI

The Virtue of Compassion

My dear brothers and sisters: as we celebrate this Marian Year in preparation for the third millennium of Christianity, let us join the Mother of God in her pilgrimage of faith. Let us learn *the virtue of compassion* from her whose heart was pierced with a sword at the foot of the Cross. It is the virtue that prompted the Good Samaritan to stop beside the victim on the road, rather than to continue on or to cross over to the other side. Whether it be the case of the person next to us or of distant peoples and nations, we must be Good Samaritans to all those who suffer. We must be the compassionate "neighbor" of those in need, not only when it is emotionally rewarding or convenient, but also when it is demanding and inconvenient.[1] Compassion is a virtue we cannot neglect in a world in which the human suffering of so many of our brothers and sisters is needlessly increased by oppression, deprivation, and underdevelopment—by poverty, hunger, and disease. Compassion is also called for in the face of the spiritual emptiness and aimlessness that people can often experience amid material prosperity and comfort in developed countries such as your own. Compassion is a virtue that brings healing to those who bestow it, not only in this present life but in eternity: "Blessed are they who show mercy, mercy shall be theirs" (Mt 5:7).

Through the faith of Mary, then, let us fix our gaze on *the mystery of Christ*. The mystery of the Son of Man, written in the earthly history of humanity, is at the same time the definitive manifestation of God in that history.

Simeon says: "This child is destined to be the downfall and the rise of many in Israel, a sign that will be opposed" (Lk 2:34). How profound these words are! How far down these words reach into the history of man! Into the history of us all: Christ is destined for the ruin and the resurrection of many! Christ is a sign of contradiction! Is this not also true in our time? In our age? *In our generation?*

And standing next to Christ is Mary. To her Simeon says: ". . . so that the thoughts of many hearts may be laid bare. And you yourself shall be pierced with a sword" (Lk 2:35).

Today we ask for *humility of heart* and for a clear
    conscience:
before God
through Christ.
Yes, we ask that the thoughts of our hearts may be
laid bare. We ask that our *consciences may be pure*:
before God
through the Cross of Christ
in the heart of Mary. Amen.

— Excerpt from homily given at the Coliseum
in Los Angeles on September 15, 1987

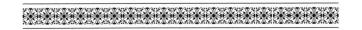

XVII

The Mysteries of Light

Moving on from the infancy and the hidden life in Nazareth to the public life of Jesus, our contemplation brings us to those mysteries which may be called in a special way "mysteries of light." Certainly the whole mystery of Christ is a mystery of light. He is the "light of the world" (Jn 8:12). Yet this truth emerges in a special way during the years of his public life, when he proclaims the Gospel of the Kingdom. In proposing to the Christian community five significant moments—"luminous" mysteries—during this phase of Christ's life, I think that the following can be fittingly singled out: (1) his Baptism in the

Jordan, (2) his self-manifestation at the wedding of Cana, (3) his proclamation of the Kingdom of God, with his call to conversion, (4) his Transfiguration, and finally, (5) his institution of the Eucharist, as the sacramental expression of the Paschal Mystery.

Each of these mysteries is *a revelation of the Kingdom now present in the very person of Jesus.* The Baptism in the Jordan is first of all a mystery of light. Here, as Christ descends into the waters, the innocent one who became "sin" for our sake (cf. 2 Cor 5:21), the heavens open wide and the voice of the Father declares him the beloved Son (cf. Mt 3:17 and parallels), while the Spirit descends on him to invest him with the mission which he is to carry out. Another mystery of light is the first of the signs, given at Cana (cf. Jn 2:1–12), when Christ changes water into wine and opens the hearts of the disciples to faith, thanks to the intervention of Mary, the first among believers. Another mystery of light is the preaching by which Jesus proclaims the coming of the Kingdom of God, calls to conversion (cf. Mk 1:15), and forgives the sins of all who draw near to him in humble trust (cf. Mk 2:3–13; Lk 7:47–48): the inauguration of that ministry of mercy which he continues to exercise until the end of the world, particularly through the Sacrament of Reconciliation which he has entrusted to his Church (cf. Jn 20:22–23). The mystery of light *par excellence* is the Transfiguration, traditionally believed to have taken place on Mount Tabor. The glory of the Godhead shines forth from the face of Christ as the Father commands the astonished Apostles to "listen to him" (cf. Lk 9:35 and parallels) and to prepare to experience with him the agony of the Passion, so as to come with him to the joy of the Resurrection and a life transfigured by the Holy Spirit. A final mystery of light is the institution of the Eucharist, in which Christ offers his Body and Blood as food under the signs of bread and wine, and testifies "to the end" his love for humanity (Jn 13:1), for whose salvation he will offer himself in sacrifice.

In these mysteries, apart from the miracle at Cana, *the presence of Mary remains in the background.* The Gospels make only the briefest reference to her occasional presence at one moment or other during the preaching of Jesus (cf. Mk 3:31–5; Jn 2:12), and they give no indication that she was present at the Last Supper and the institution of the Eucharist. Yet the role she assumed at Cana in some way accompanies Christ throughout his ministry. The revelation made directly by the Father at the Baptism in the Jordan and echoed by John the Baptist is placed upon Mary's lips at Cana, and it becomes the great maternal counsel which Mary addresses to the Church of every age: "Do whatever he tells you" (Jn 2:5). This counsel is a fitting introduction to the words and signs of Christ's public ministry and it forms the Marian foundation of all the "mysteries of light."

— Excerpt from Apostolic Letter *Rosarium Virginis Mariae*, no. 21, October 16, 2002

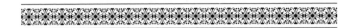

XVIII

Jesus, the Good Shepherd

Who is the God whose glory we desire to proclaim by means of the Eucharist?

He is the God who shows us the way of salvation. Thus the Psalmist, who urges all the nations of the earth to praise the glory of God, at the same time exclaims: "may your ways be known upon earth; among all nations your salvation" (Ps 67:3). Our God shows us the way. He is not the God of intellectual abstraction, but *the God of the Covenant, the God of salvation, the Good Shepherd*.

Christ, the Son of the living God, speaks to us this very day in the Gospel, using this word, so simple yet so eloquent and rich: *Shepherd! "I am the Good Shepherd,"* he says. "I know my sheep and my sheep know me in the same way that the Father knows me and I know the Father" (Jn 10:14–15). In another passage of the Gospel Christ says to us: "No one knows the Son but the Father, and no one knows the Father but the Son— and anyone to whom the Son wishes to reveal him" (Mt 11:27). *The Son, Jesus Christ*, is the Shepherd precisely *because he reveals the Father to us*. He is the Good Shepherd. And the Father is our Shepherd. And the Father is our Shepherd through the Son, through Christ. And in his Son the Father wants us to have eternal life.

Jesus goes on to tell us, in words that speak eloquently of his deep love for us: *"The Good Shepherd lays down his life for the sheep"* (Jn 10:11).

Who is this God whose truth we desire to confess by means of the Eucharist? He is the Father who in Christ gives life to us whom he created in his own image and likeness. This *life in God is salvation*. It is liberation from death. It is redemption from our sins. And this God is *Christ*, the Son who is of one substance with the Father, who became man for us and for our salvation, Christ the Good Shepherd who has *given his very own life for the sheep*.

The Eucharist proclaims this truth about God. The Sacrament of the Body and Blood of Christ is offered as a redemptive sacrifice for the sins of the world. It is the sacrament of the Death and Resurrection of Christ, *in which our new life in God begins*.

This God is Love. The Good Shepherd expresses this truth about God. More than the truth, he expresses the very *reality of God as Love.* Love desires what is good. It desires salvation. It is "gentle and patient," and it "will have no end" (cf. 1 Cor 13:4–8). It will not rest *before it has nourished and given life to all* in the great sheepfold, before it has embraced all. For this reason Jesus says: "I have other sheep that do not belong to this fold. I must lead them, too, and they shall hear my voice. There shall be one flock then, one shepherd" (Jn 10:16).

— Excerpt from homily given at Tamiami Park, Miami, on September 11, 1987

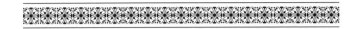

XIX

Allow the Holy Spirit to Work in You

When Mary realized who it was that was calling her, all fear was banished and she replied: *"I am the servant of the Lord. Let it be done to me as you say"* (Lk 1:38). And at that instant, she became the Mother of the Son of God. This is the extraordinary truth that we meditate on in the first mystery of the Rosary, the Annunciation.

All this happened so that, as Saint Paul says, *we might be redeemed and might receive adoption as God's sons and daughters* (cf. Gal 4:5). In Christ, the Holy Spirit makes us God's beloved children. The Incarnation of the Son of God happened once, and is unrepeatable. Divine adoption goes on all the time, through the Church, the Body of Christ, and particularly through the Sacraments, through Baptism, Penance, the Eucharist, and of course the Sacrament of Pentecost that we call Confirmation. And then Saint Paul writes something very striking: *the proof that we are God's children is that he "has sent forth into our hearts the Spirit of his Son, which cries out 'Abba!' ('Father!')"* (Gal 4:6). *Abba! Father!* This is our prayer every time we say the Our Father. But we have to say it in the Spirit, with a clear awareness that in Christ "we are no longer slaves but children, and therefore heirs with Christ to his kingdom" (cf. Gal 4:7). This new condition of ours as Christians, that is, our transformation through grace and our sharing in divine life itself, will reach its fulfillment in eternity. Then we shall share the happiness with which God himself is happy, Father, Son, and Holy Spirit. Do you see how important it is to invoke the Holy Spirit and to allow him to work in us? We must remember that the Holy Spirit can do great things for us! And the Holy Spirit does great things for us every day.

— Excerpt from homily to young people in Central Park,
New York City, October 7, 1995

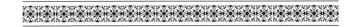

XX

Do Not Be Discouraged

The Gospel of Jesus Christ is not a private opinion, a remote spiritual ideal, or a mere program for personal growth. The Gospel is the power which can transform the world! The Gospel is no abstraction: it is the living person of Jesus Christ, the Word of God, the reflection of the Father's glory (cf. Heb 1:2), the Incarnate Son who reveals the deepest meaning of our humanity and the noble destiny to which the whole human family is called.[1] Christ has commanded us to let the light of the Gospel shine forth in our service to society. How can we profess faith in God's word, and then refuse to let it inspire and direct our thinking, our activity, our decisions, and our responsibilities toward one another? . . .

Today though, some Catholics are tempted to discouragement or disillusionment, like the prophet Habakkuk in the First Reading. They are tempted to cry out to the Lord in a different way: why does God not intervene when violence threatens his people; why does God let us see ruin and misery; why does God permit evil? Like the prophet Habakkuk, and like the thirsty Israelites in the desert at Meribah and Massah, our trust can falter; we can lose patience with God. In the drama of history, we can find our dependence upon God burdensome rather than liberating. We too can "harden our hearts."

And yet the prophet gives us an answer to our impatience: "If God delays, wait for him; he will surely come, he will not be late" (cf. Hab 2:3). A Polish proverb expresses the same conviction in another way: *"God takes his time, but he is just."* Our waiting for God is never in vain. Every moment is our opportunity to model ourselves on Jesus Christ—to allow the power of the Gospel to transform our personal lives and our service to others, according to the spirit of the Beatitudes. "Bear your share of the hardship which the Gospel entails," writes Paul to Timothy in today's Second Reading (2 Tim 1:8). This is no idle exhortation to endurance. No, it is an invitation to enter more deeply into the *Christian vocation* which belongs to us all by

Baptism. There is no evil to be faced that Christ does not face with us. There is no enemy that Christ has not already conquered. There is no cross to bear that Christ has not already borne for us, and does not now bear with us. And on the far side of every cross we find the newness of life in the Holy Spirit, that new life which will reach its fulfillment in the resurrection. This is our *faith*. This is our *witness* before the world.

— Excerpt from homily given in Baltimore,
Oriole Park at Camden Yards, October 8, 1995

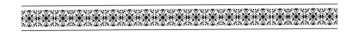

XXI

The Beatitudes:
The Way of Holiness

Today's liturgy speaks completely of holiness. But to know what is the way to holiness, we must go with the Apostles up the mount of the Beatitudes to draw near to Jesus and listen to the words of life that come from his lips. Today too he says to us again:

"Blessed are the poor in spirit, for theirs is the kingdom of heaven!" The divine Teacher proclaims "blessed" and, we could say, "canonizes" first of all the poor in spirit, that is, those whose heart is free of prejudices and conditionings, and who are therefore totally disposed to the divine will.

Their total and trusting fidelity to God presupposes renunciation and consistent self-detachment.

Blessed are those who mourn! This is the blessedness not only of those who suffer from the many misfortunes that belong to the mortal human condition, but also those who courageously accept the sufferings that result from the sincere profession of Gospel morality.

Blessed are the pure in heart! He proclaims blessed those who are not content with outward or ritual purity, but seek that absolute inner rectitude which excludes all deceit and duplicity.

Blessed are those who hunger and thirst for righteousness! Human righteousness is already a very lofty goal, which ennobles the heart of whoever pursues it, but Jesus is thinking of that greater righteousness which lies in seeking God's saving will: blessed above all are those who hunger and thirst for this righteousness. For Jesus says: "He who does the will of my Father who is in heaven shall enter the kingdom of heaven" (Mt 7:21).

Blessed are the merciful! Happy are those who overcome their hardness of heart and indifference, to recognize in practice the primacy of compassionate love, following the example of the Good Samaritan and, in the last analysis, of the Father "rich in mercy" (Eph 2:4).

Blessed are the peacemakers! Peace, the sum of all messianic blessings, is a demanding task. In a world marked by tremendous antagonisms and barriers, fraternal harmony inspired by love and sharing must be promoted by overcoming hostilities and conflicts. Blessed are those who dedicate themselves to this most noble endeavor!

The saints took these words of Jesus seriously. They believed that they would find "happiness" by putting them into practice in their lives. And they realized their truth in everyday experience: despite their trials, moments of darkness and failures, they already tasted here below the deep joy of communion with Christ. In him they discovered the initial seed, already present in time, of the future glory of God's Kingdom.

— Excerpt from homily given on All Saints Day,
November 1, 2000

XXII

The Gospel of Life

At the end of this chapter, in which we have reflected on the Christian message about life, I would like to pause with each one of you to *contemplate the One who was pierced* and who draws all people to himself (cf. Jn 19:37; 12:32). Looking at "the spectacle" of the Cross (cf. Lk 23:48) we shall discover in this glorious tree the fulfillment and the complete revelation of the whole *Gospel of life*.

In the early afternoon of Good Friday, "there was darkness over the whole land . . . while the sun's light failed; and the curtain of the temple was torn in two" (Lk 23:44, 45). This is the symbol of a great cosmic disturbance and a massive conflict between the forces of good and the forces of evil, between life and death. Today we too find ourselves in the midst of a dramatic conflict between the "culture of death" and the "culture of life." But the glory of the Cross is not overcome by this darkness; rather, it shines forth ever more radiantly and brightly and is revealed as the center, meaning, and goal of all history and of every human life.

Jesus is nailed to the cross and is lifted up from the earth. He experiences the moment of his greatest "powerlessness," and his life seems completely delivered to the derision of his adversaries and into the hands of his executioners: he is mocked, jeered at, insulted (cf. Mk 15:24–36). And yet, precisely amid all this, having seen him breathe his last, the Roman centurion exclaims: "Truly this man was the Son of God!" (Mk 15:39) It is thus, at the moment of his greatest weakness, that the Son of God is revealed for who he is: *on the Cross his glory is made manifest.*

By his death, Jesus sheds light on the meaning of the life and death of every human being. Before he dies, Jesus prays to the Father, asking forgiveness for his persecutors (cf. Lk 23:34), and to the criminal who asks him to remember him in his kingdom he replies: "Truly, I say to you, today you will be with me in paradise" (Lk 23:43). After his death "the tombs also were opened, and many bodies of the saints who had fallen asleep were raised" (Mt 27:52). The salvation wrought by Jesus is the bestowal of life and resurrection. Throughout his earthly life, Jesus had indeed bestowed salvation by healing and doing good to all (cf. Acts 10:38). But his miracles, healings, and even his raising of the dead were signs of another salvation, a salvation which consists in the forgiveness of sins, that is, in setting man free from his greatest sickness and in raising him to the very life of God.

On the Cross, the miracle of the serpent lifted up by Moses in the desert (Jn 3:14–15; cf. Num 21:8–9) is renewed and brought to full and definitive perfection. Today too, by looking upon the one who was pierced, every person whose life is threatened encounters the sure hope of finding freedom and redemption.

— Excerpt from Encyclical Letter *Evangelium Vitae*,
no. 50, March 25, 1995

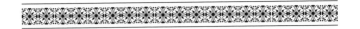

XXIII

Message to Athletes

"*Those that sow in tears shall reap rejoicing*" (Ps 125:5). The responsorial psalm reminded us that *persevering effort is needed to succeed in life.* Anyone who plays sports knows this very well: it is only at the cost of strenuous training that significant results are achieved. The athlete, therefore, agrees with the psalmist when he says that the effort spent in sowing finds its reward in the joy of the harvest: "Although they go forth weeping, carrying the seed to be sown, they shall come back rejoicing, carrying their sheaves" (Ps 125:6).

At the recent Olympic games in Sydney we admired the feats of the great athletes, who sacrificed themselves for years, day after day, to achieve those results. This is *the logic of sport,* especially Olympic sports; it is also *the logic of life*: without sacrifices, important results are not obtained, or even genuine satisfaction.

Once again the Apostle Paul has reminded us of this: "Every athlete exercises self-control in all things. They do it to receive a perishable wreath, but we an imperishable" (1 Cor 9:25). Every Christian is called to become a strong *athlete of Christ,* that is, a faithful and courageous witness to his Gospel. But to succeed in this, he must persevere in prayer, be trained in virtue, and follow the divine Master in everything.

He, in fact, *is God's true athlete*: Christ is the "more powerful" Man (cf. Mk 1:7), who for our sake confronted and defeated the "opponent," Satan, by the power of the Holy Spirit, thus inaugurating the Kingdom of God. He teaches us that, to enter into glory, we must undergo suffering (cf. Lk 24:26, 46); he has gone before us on this path, so that we might follow in his footsteps.

— Excerpt from a message to athletes
on the Jubilee of Sports People, October 29, 2000

Saint Thérèse of Lisieux and the Vocation to Love

Everyone . . . realizes that today something surprising is happening. Saint Thérèse of Lisieux was unable to attend a university or engage in systematic study. She died young: nevertheless, from this day forward she will be honored as a doctor of the Church, an outstanding recognition which raises her in the esteem of the entire Christian community far beyond any academic title.

Indeed, when the Magisterium proclaims someone a doctor of the Church, it intends to point out to all the faithful, particularly to those who perform in the Church the fundamental service of preaching or who undertake the delicate task of theological teaching and research, that the doctrine professed and proclaimed by a certain person can be a reference point, not only because it conforms to revealed truth, but also because it sheds new light on the mysteries of the faith, a deeper understanding of Christ's mystery. The Council reminded us that, with the help of the Holy Spirit, understanding of the "*depositum fidei*" continually grows in the Church, and not only does the richly contemplative study to which theologians are called, not only does the Magisterium of pastors, endowed with the "sure charism of truth," contribute to this growth process, but also that "*profound understanding of spiritual things*" which is given *through experience*, with the wealth and diversity of gifts, to all those who let themselves be docilely led by God's Spirit.[1] *Lumen Gentium*, for its part, teaches that God himself "speaks to us" (no. 50) in his saints. It is for this reason that the spiritual experience of the saints has a special value for deepening our knowledge of the divine mysteries, which remain ever greater than our thoughts, and not by chance does the Church choose only saints to be distinguished with the title of "doctor."

Thérèse of the Child Jesus and the Holy Face is the youngest of all the "doctors of the Church," but her ardent spiritual journey shows such maturity, and the insights of faith expressed in her writings are so vast and profound that they deserve a place among the great spiritual masters.

In the Apostolic Letter which I wrote for this occasion, I stressed several salient aspects of her doctrine. But how can we fail to recall here what can be considered its high point, starting with the account of the moving discovery of her special vocation in the Church? "Charity," she wrote, "gave me the key to my vocation. I understood that if the Church had a body composed of different members, the most necessary and most noble of all could not be lacking to it, and so I understood that the Church had a heart and that this heart was burning with love. I understood that it was love alone that made the Church's members act, that if love were ever extinguished, apostles would not proclaim the Gospel and martyrs would refuse to shed their blood. I understood that love includes all vocations. . . . Then in the excess of my delirious joy, I cried out: 'O Jesus, my Love . . . at last I have found my vocation; my vocation is Love!'"[2] This is a wonderful passage which suffices itself to show that one can apply to Saint Thérèse the Gospel passage we heard in the Liturgy of the Word: "I thank you, Father, Lord of heaven and earth, because you have hidden these things from the wise and the intelligent and have revealed them to infants" (Mt 11:25).

Thérèse of Lisieux did not only grasp and describe the profound truth of Love as the center and heart of the

Church, but in her short life she lived it intensely. It is precisely this *convergence of doctrine and concrete experience*, of truth and life, of teaching and practice, which shines with particular brightness in this saint, and which makes her an attractive model especially for young people and for those who are seeking true meaning for their life.

Before the emptiness of so many words, Thérèse offers another solution, the one Word of salvation which, understood and lived in silence, becomes a source of renewed life. She counters a rational culture, so often overcome by practical materialism, with the disarming simplicity of the "little way" which, by returning to the essentials, leads to the secret of all life: the divine Love that surrounds and penetrates every human venture. In a time like ours, so frequently marked by an ephemeral and hedonistic culture, this new doctor of the Church proves to be remarkably effective in enlightening the mind and heart of those who hunger and thirst for truth and love.

Saint Thérèse is presented as a doctor of the Church on the day we are celebrating World Mission Sunday. She had the ardent desire to dedicate herself to proclaiming the Gospel, and she would have liked to have crowned her witness with the supreme sacrifice of martyrdom.[3] Moreover, her intense personal commitment supporting the apostolic work of Fr. Maurice Bellière and Fr. Adolphe Rulland, missionaries respectively in Africa and China, is well-known. In her zealous love for evangelization, Thérèse had one ideal, as she herself says: "What we ask of him is to work for his glory, to love him and to make him loved."[4]

The way she took to reach this ideal of life is not that of the great undertakings reserved for the few, but on the contrary, a way within everyone's reach, the "little way," a path of trust and total self-abandonment to the Lord's grace. It is not a prosaic way, as if it were less demanding. It is in fact a demanding reality, as the Gospel always is. But it is a way in which one is imbued with a sense of trusting abandonment to divine mercy, which makes even the most rigorous spiritual commitment light.

Because of this way in which she receives everything as "grace," because she puts her relationship with Christ and her choice of love at the center of everything, because of the place she gives to the ardent impulses of the heart on her spiritual journey, Thérèse of Lisieux is a saint who remains young despite the passing years, and she is held up as an eminent model and guide on the path of Christians....

Yes, O Father, we bless you, together with Jesus (cf. Mt 11:25), because you have "hidden your secrets from the wise and the intelligent" and have revealed them to this "little one" whom today you hold up again for our attention and imitation.

Thank you for the wisdom you gave her, making her an exceptional witness and teacher of life for the whole Church!

Thank you for the love you poured out upon her and which continues to illumine and warm hearts, spurring them to holiness.

The desire Thérèse expressed to "spend her heaven doing good on earth"[5] continues to be fulfilled in a marvelous way.

Thank you, Father, for making her close to us today with a new title, to the praise and glory of your name for ever and ever. Amen!

— Excerpt from homily given on October 19, 1997, when Saint Thérèse was proclaimed a Doctor of the Church

Notes

II

1. Cf. Gen 3:22 concerning the "tree of life"; cf. also Jn 3:36; 4:14; 5:24; 6:40, 47; 10:28; 12:50; 14:6; Acts 13:48; Rom 6:23; Gal 6:8; 1 Tim 1:16; Tit 1:2; 3:7; 1 Pet 3:22; 1 Jn 1:2; 2:25; 5:11, 13; Rev 2:7.

2. Cf. Saint Thomas Aquinas, *Summa Theol.*, Ia–IIae, q. 80, a. 4, ad 3.

3. *De Civitate Dei*, XIV, 28: *CCL* 48, p. 541.

4. Pastoral Constitution on the Church in the Modern World, *Gaudium et Spes*, no. 36.

IV

1. *Diary*, Libreria Editrice Vaticana, p. 132.

2. Ibid., p. 374.

3. Cf. *Dives in Misericordia*, no. 7.

4. Ibid., no. 14.

V

1. Cf. Eucharistic Prayer IV.

2. Cf. Vatican Council II: Pastoral Constitution on the Church in the Modern World, *Gaudium et Spes*, no. 37: *AAS* 58 (1966), 1054–1055; Dogmatic Constitution on the Church, *Lumen Gentium*, no. 48: *AAS* 57 (1965), 53–54.

3. Cf. Saint Thomas, *Summa Theol.*, 111, q. 46, a. 1, ad 3.

VI

1. The Nicene-Constantinopolitan Creed.

VIII

1. Cf. Sequence *Veni, Sancte Spiritus*.

2. Saint Bonaventure, *De Septem Donis Spiritus Sancti, Collatio* II, 3: *Ad Claras Aquas*, V, 463.

XVI

1. Cf. John Paul II, *Salvifici Doloris*, nos. 28–30.

XX

1. Cf. *Gaudium et Spes*, no. 22.

XXIV

1. Cf. *Dei Verbum*, no. 8.

2. *Ms B*, 3v°.

3. Cf. *Ms B*, 3r°.

4. *Letter* 220.

5. *Opere* Complete, p. 1050.

A Note on Sources

The source of each excerpt is noted immediately following each selection. All of these encyclicals, apostolic letters, homilies, etc. can be found on the Vatican website: www.vatican.va.

BOOKS & MEDIA

The Daughters of St. Paul operate book and media centers at the following addresses. Visit, call, or write the one nearest you today, or find us at www.pauline.org.

CALIFORNIA

3908 Sepulveda Blvd, Culver City, CA 90230	310-397-8676
935 Brewster Avenue, Redwood City, CA 94063	650-369-4230
5945 Balboa Avenue, San Diego, CA 92111	858-565-9181

FLORIDA

145 S.W. 107th Avenue, Miami, FL 33174	305-559-6715

HAWAII

1143 Bishop Street, Honolulu, HI 96813	808-521-2731
Neighbor Islands call:	866-521-2731

ILLINOIS

172 North Michigan Avenue, Chicago, IL 60601	312-346-4228

LOUISIANA

4403 Veterans Memorial Blvd, Metairie, LA 70006	504-887-7631

MASSACHUSETTS

885 Providence Hwy, Dedham, MA 02026	781-326-5385

MISSOURI

9804 Watson Road, St. Louis, MO 63126	314-965-3512

NEW YORK

64 W. 38th Street, New York, NY 10018	212-754-1110

PENNSYLVANIA

Philadelphia—relocating	215-676-9494

SOUTH CAROLINA

243 King Street, Charleston, SC 29401	843-577-0175

VIRGINIA

1025 King Street, Alexandria, VA 22314	703-549-3806

CANADA

3022 Dufferin Street, Toronto, ON M6B 3T5	416-781-9131

¡También somos su fuente para libros,
videos y música en español!